DAUGHTERS OF THE HOUSE

First published in 2019 by
The Dedalus Press
13 Moyclare Road
Baldoyle
Dublin D13 K1C2
Ireland

www.**dedaluspress**.com

Copyright © Catherine Phil MacCarthy, 2019

ISBN 978 1 910251 52 2 paperback
ISBN 978 1 910251 53 9 hardback

All rights reserved.
No part of this publication may be reproduced in any form
or by any means without the prior permission
of the publisher.

The moral right of the author has been asserted.

Dedalus Press titles are available in Ireland
from Argosy Books (argosybooks.ie) and in the UK
from Inpress Books (www.inpressbooks.co.uk)

Cover image: *Climate Bell 3,* 2016, by Vivienne Roche,
sculpture in cast bronze, 28 x 10 x 10 cms.
www.vivienneroche.com

The Dedalus Press receives financial assistance from
The Arts Council / An Chomhairle Ealaíon.

DAUGHTERS OF THE HOUSE

CATHERINE PHIL MacCARTHY

DEDALUS PRESS

Contents

Singer / 9
Now I See Them Everywhere / 11
Île de la Cité / 13
Sunset on *La Tour Eiffel* / 14
The Bells of Notre Dame / 15
Jardins des Plantes / 16
Evacuation / 17
The Suitcase / 18
Lá Fhéile Pádraig / 19
Salon des Indépendants, 1884 / 20
A Marketable Craft / 21
Paris Diary / 22
Sarah Purser's *Lady with a Monkey, A Portrait* / 23
The Meeting / 24
Daughters of the House, O'Halloran's Fort / 25
Land League Cottage / 27
Wedding Song / 30
Venus del Pendo / 31
Letter to Sarah Purser: 19.12.1888 / 32
Inghinidhe na hÉireann / 33
Two Portraits, Michael Davitt / 34
Legacies of Empire / 35
Brigantium / 36
21, rue Bonaparte / 37
Maiden Voyage / 38
Wounds / 39
Surgeons & Insurgents / 40
Painter's Model / 41
Guinea Fowl / 42
Digital Archive / 43
Binn Éadair, En Plein Air / 44

Harry Clarke's *Gobnait* / 45
Magu and the Deer / 46
Before the Solstice / 47
Adam / 48
Eostre and Hare / 49
Fledglings / 50
Sea Swallows / 51
Prodigal / 52
Coral / 53
Women Only / 54
Nightingale's Song / 55
Riverrun / 56
Tosca / 57
Traders / 58
The Habit / 59
I Want to Hold Your Hand / 60
The Hat / 61
Like a Miniature Chillida / 62
Presence / 63
Wave Riders / 64
Arrival / 65
The Chamber / 66

NOTES / 67

for my family

&

for Thomas O'Grady and Katie Conboy

Singer

Along Rue Lacépède, a window on shoes
and leather belts. Inside the door,
the rich odour.

A man, at a counter, lays aside his work,
displays shoes he makes himself
for dancing, classical jazz.

'Pelure' is the word that he suggests,
offering to fit a waist. I think of live calves.
Vellum. The Book of Kells. My father

choosing a belly-band for a horse
at Carews, William Street,
a new 'winkers' for the mare.

There, tools are clipped on a wall.
Here again, the gilt-embossed *S*
on a black sewing machine,

its wrought-iron treadle spells
S-I-N-G-E-R. Monsieur praises
the invention, shows the needle's eye.

There's my mother at the table
hand winding the wheel,
her mouth full of pins,

rat-tat-tat of the silvery metal foot
between mid-finger and index.
The needle drills a long seam

to sew a new dress, a summer shift,
a dancing skirt in green poplin,
the bobbin spinning. Fabric

cascades onto the floor,
a waterfall spilling from a bolt
across the table. All business,

new words drop from her lips,
'muslin', 'chiffon', 'bias',
'tension.'

Now I See Them Everywhere

The first, five years ago at a display
in the crowded marquee,
potted, sturdy, deep green,

fan-shaped leaf
asking to be brought home.
I balked at lifting the weight

and carrying it through the throng,
across the open field,
our city veldt.

When I saw the second
last December, leaves, a lemon yellow
against the azure sky,

my regret loomed.
If I started now, how long would it take
to grow one that high?

The metal tag said: *Gingko biloba, 1811.*
The reign of Napoléon.
Planted in a corner of 'Jardins du Roi'.

All this time, it has seen summers
come and go. Comets.
Earthquakes. Wars.

Animals in the 'Ménagerie'.
How does it mind the long years,
of locals who stood

in its humble shadow, Becquerel,
Henri Rousseau, Madame Curie?
The third, I came across in Kew.

That brings me to the Dutch
in search of spice,
where seeds fetched hands,

gardens in the West.
The sapling on my lawn warns:
All manifestations are temporary.

Each one you see of me is a replica.
All day I look at a path.
I am a doorway through the Ice,

a window on Hiroshima,
a seedling fossilized in rock
that preserves me.

Île de la Cité

We descend the hill – across
Rue des Écoles, down to the quays
onto Les Îles, beyond the boundary
of Notre-Dame – find ourselves
strolling over Pont de l'Archevêché,
rails a tapestry of locks,
notice each other out of place
in the chill December wind.
You stroll on past tacky declarations

bedecked with ribbons, scrawled hearts.
Two thousand locks gleam in the sun.
They nod to Abélard and Héloïse.
Where, the lovers who made
promises in stealth? Keys rust
on the riverbed of the Seine,
while a ferry, the *Isabelle Adjani*,
glides above. I walk on, past
vows sworn to last, to where
you wait for me, not looking back.

Sunset on *La Tour Eiffel*

Inside the windproof lattice
of girders, bolted with countless rivets
that crisscross up to a thousand feet
in the freezing air, at the summit
we stand and stare at the horizon
as the clock melts off the rim
leaking dyes through smog.
Earth turns on this clear solstice
to greet a rising half–moon
and lone star in the east.

From the wire mesh up here,
traffic is a yellow river
streaming through grey *quartiers*.
One by one, the monuments are lit,
Les Invalides, *L'Arc de Triomphe*,
La Défense, a virtual Manhattan.
Beside the moon, Jupiter burns bright,
eye of the night staring across distance
at humans gazing from the pyramid
of a kingdom, curious and wired.

The Bells of Notre Dame

Nine bells line the main aisle,
flaxen domes echo one another;
visitors pour in,
rocked by each
newborn colossus
stood on oak beams,
cast in bronze with
its own design
and tone.

'Marie', 'Gabriel', 'Denis',
parade along the queue –
'Et elle conçu du Saint Esprit.'
Hands caress the patina,
gauge the width
of the lip, test notes
rapping the rim.
Each chime stirs
the house

with an acoustic tone
spins a celebratory hum
of pandemonium,
heralds the North tower
hung with instruments again,
that mark the flow of hours
for how long more
from earth
across the skies?

Jardins des Plantes

This one standing alone
at the border of a lawn
is ochre-yellow. Fan-shaped
blades float down luminous,
one at a time, in winter sun,
like miniature wafer-thin
cross-sections of the brain,
or an unvoiced name
that rustles on the tongue.
Hear the subtle acoustic
of loss, off high branches
and bracts, a papery sound
in the chill, blue Sunday air.

Each pendant leaf resists
gravity, a silken lobe
echoes codes over
generations to the era
of the dinosaurs. The fall
exposes deeply fissured bark,
arc of ascending limbs,
and a blonde cascade
at base of the trunk,
and, who knows,
after our human world is gone
may transmit this wordless
lexicon of fruition?

Evacuation

Between La Courneuve and Le Bourget
a silent village sprang up overnight.
Shack after shack. On grass margins
by the wire fence of the rail-line,
a township multiplies.
MDF boards raise walls, and roofs
held down with suitcases and prams.

Mothers in long skirts wear babes on hips.
Bare-chested men sport deltoid tattoos.
Couples in traditional dress meet
at clubs in local suburbs after dark.
They practise needlework,
sing *sean nós*, dance flamenco.
Where do they go in the freezing fog?

No tots by campfires, no teens play in gangs.
A mattress, or two, and bicycles strewn.
On radio, historians mythologise:
'Kale', 'Sinti', 'Romanichal', 'Gypsy'.
Hungarian Dances of Franz Liszt.
Moulin Rouge, Can-can, La Belle Époque.
Drawings of Toulouse-Lautrec.

The Suitcase

He arrived with a gun-metal blue valise,
patterned in silver stripes
weighing twenty-two kilos,

name and destination
in gilt letters across the lid.

Mother placed in his hand
an envelope of folded newspaper
with lotus, hibiscus, cherry and roses,

aromas of Karaikal offered to the gods for his safety;
inside the satin blue lining,
holy pictures of Shiva and Parvati,

a tiny, green, cardboard calendar.
Towels were a gift from Father,
the colour of French and Indian flags
and a hoe-shaped Wilkinson Sword razor.

He brought a small stack of clothes,
Indian cotton, new for the journey,

a copybook with ivory pages,
his repertoire of French words
written in pencil with Hindi translations.

And the photograph so that
he would never forget his parents.

Lá Fhéile Pádraig

They stood in the aisle
after hearing Ó'Riada's Aifreann

sung in Notre-Dame for the first time,
the soloist heard in the light of

gothic stained-glass,
North and South Rose windows.

Irish from Brittany to Aquitaine,
visitors claiming ancestry –

Boston, Sydney, Rio, West Clare –
wove along the crowded nave

trying to see where the shamrock,
sent in clumps from home,

was given out in clusters,
sprigs passed from hand to hand,

divided, shared, threaded through
buttonholes, brooches, hats,

while outside, in the cold, bells rang loud,
companions spread across the Seine

and falling from stems
for the rest of that afternoon,

seeds from Kildare, onto French ground –
particles of Irish clay.

Salon des Indépendants, 1884

She went to Champs-Élysées, that first show,
found names, Degas, Monet, Berthe Morisot,
artists the world did not yet value.

A Marketable Craft

after 'In the Studio' by Marie Bashkirtseff

You are not in the frame at Julian's –
for this is eighteen-eighty-one –
though here she is

with colleagues crowded in
to that tubercular attic on the fifth floor
off Boulevard des Capucines.

The carmine, velvet cloak is cast aside.
Slate-blue apron, ankle-length dress –
a few wear hats or lace bonnets.

They prop canvas against easel, or chair,
make do: charcoal, tablet;
knife, mixing board.

Before all, stands the nude boy.
Beside him, a skeleton looks down.
The *atelier* clock tells Paris Mean Time.

Daughters of nerve, of gentle birth
and foreign tongue, create the world
and draw from eight to five, with those

on the bread-line famished at night.
La Dame aux Camélias haunts her
dreams. Figures on canvas gibe.

Paris Diary

Once she found herself back at the heart
of this ancient city, in the silence of
her third-floor room that overlooked

an inner courtyard with only birds
to listen to in the early morning, distant
traffic along medieval streets, words

written long ago echoed a sacred vow:
I need but two dark blouses a year,
a change of linen that I could wash myself,

the simplest food fresh from the garden
and the means to work; this is all.
The omnibus, or to go about on foot.

Sarah Purser's *Lady with a Monkey, A Portrait*

Though high and solitary, she is not yet stern.
Her arms rest on a carved buffet,
enfold a black monkey, its face and eyes

a cameo of pensiveness. At first glance,
it's all about the dress: metallic silk
lamé falling to the floor, richly embroidered.

At twenty-three, Miss Gonne looks out
from under the high crown of a russet hat
with upturned brim and net

that perches to one side of her head.
Auburn hair flowers from the nape
in a rosette. She appears

girl become woman, already in love,
choosing her state, beyond snobbery
and wealth, her privileges scant defence

against heartbreak. Does she speak
of her time in Falcarragh, decrees
made in court? A mother and four children,

sleeping by the road. Emergency men
with battering ram, smashing down doors.
Cries of a newborn, locked in her throat.

The Meeting

'Is it not the aim of painting to copy nature?' – Marie Bashkirtseff

Hard to say if it's a bird's nest –

heads close together, a group of boys,
the youngest, maybe six, hands clasped behind him,
the eldest, satchel slung across his shoulder,
his back to the viewer, holds

what could as well be a twig, a broken fishing rod,
or archery bow. They cluster in a circle
at the street corner in smocks and shoes
that suggest they're on the way home from school.

Manly solidarity and easy camaraderie
raises a question that extends to the plaited,
dark-haired girl at the margins of the canvas
in pinafore and blue apron –

walking alone, out of the picture.

Daughters of the House, O'Halloran's Fort

We disappeared into the house
built by our own wit,
two storeys backed to the hill,
cradled in ash trees, the holding
handed down for centuries,

deep inside – stone walls,
tongue-and-groove floors,
and slated roof, windows and doors
battened tight with logs,
the eastern gable with clay,

our peaceful fort, ready for storm.
All June we were its eyes and ears,
drew water from the pump
in gallons, filled pots and churns,
came and went by a plank

through an upstairs window,
new door for walking into summer,
hay saved in the meadow,
bog irises in bloom amid rushes,
groves of whitethorn and willow.

That morning we woke at dawn,
with no delay, each to a station.
When noise went up
along the road, we knew
the party was approaching

down the slope, a procession,
bailiffs on horses, soldiers and policemen,

a great crowd of onlookers,
dog roses in bloom and wild woodbine,
foxgloves shedding their tresses.

An hour we held fast against them.
As time wore on, loud cheers from
those who climbed the ditch
and stood on boundary fences
grew deafening. In the silence after,

I listened to swallows nested
in the eaves, time to take with me
moorhens in the callow,
flocks of starling making a breeze
at dusk in the air above our heads.

No living here, for many of us?
The path was clear from the beginning.

Land League Cottage

i. Nocturne

I often woke in storm-black nights to find him
gone or working on legal papers,

changes drafted for negotiations,
his face by lamplight ghostly at table,

trim beard and brown eyes luminous
in solitary gloom, checking the words

he wrote, back to himself, each nuance.
It seemed then we were strangers anew,

his life ransom for our bankrupt country
if late evictions are gridiron to go by,

and I lifted the lid of my piano
to sound the worn ivory keys and sing –

Love's Old Sweet Song – to lull my dear
and draw him home again inside my body.

ii. Orfeo

The lodge became a peaceful cradle,
the icy clip of horseshoes down the road,

a child muttered in deepest sleep,
the sea's low murmur. No light anywhere.

Or knowing when – days, weeks – he'd come
rushing to sweep each bairn into his arm,

waving a new libretto to tease me.
Alone, I lay homesick, the Oakland house

so far away, my old bedroom. How notes
used ripple from my breast – *Che farò*

senza Euridice – the orchestra leading
the melody, our town hall full. Now all

goes on without me. I hum in darkness.
Letters take a month, bring news of friends

from choir, concerts, weddings, gossip.

iii. Aubade

The night before crossing – his maiden speech –
he laid both clothes and shoes across the chair

by the stove and tip-toed from our bed
at dawn, not to bestir me or the children,

though I lay listening to his hurried scrub
and dress and Kathleen's chesty cough,

the single spill of a blackbird's arpeggio
rending the air. His step again, soundless –

a hackney cab waiting by the gate –
his arm girded the quilt to bid farewell

in close embrace and find my lips
with lips both true and tender,

but then the chill of coat and hair.
He was soon flown –

the world of work had taken him.
Now, hear the blackbird's tune.

Wedding Song

i.m. Michael Davitt & Mary Yore 1886

The altar filled the bay window
and scents of ferns, calla lilies,

camellias, azaleas, carnations
sweetened the air – the room bedecked

for ceremony – a bridal bower.
This day was not planned for.

The inward beauty that no eyes can see
was matched in wedlock,

her young face radiant, as she took her place
beside him, who knew

leadership, despair, nobility.
The seated guests fell silent

at the sight of her entrance in white satin,
tulle veil with orange blossom,

train of lace,
his gaze lifted to receive her.

Venus del Pendo

– Museo de Prehistoria, Santander, c. 20,000 B.C.

Whose hands carved
from the antler of a deer
a female figure?
Was it even then a metaphor?
Maybe just killing time
waiting for the birth of a child.
The upward curve of her shoulder
offers an absence –
no head and face –
body, open to the skies
as if the maker ran out of space
or was called away,
other business, a forest hunt
past ash and elm that moonlit night?

The work fell between cracks,
lost in darkness for aeons
under a landslide. There
tribes once gathered
to sing out the long winter nights.
Bits of flint, bone tools,
arrowheads came to light
inside a cave deep as an underground chapel,
became clues for a man
on his knees with scalpel,
digging by the glow of burning oil,
who turned in his hands
an image that confounds.

Letter to Sarah Purser: 19.12.1888

It was indeed so kind of you to send
the box of violets, to mark ten years
of my release from Dartmoor. I had near
forgotten that, to me, eventful date.
On Saturday, I made the crossing, home.
From court, I have a month of freedom,
though not, alas, from 'Parnellism and Crime',
the drudgery that this judicial kingdom
has wrought. I must devote my holidays
to write Land League history for the trial.
I hope you're full of work, and hale,
and that your Christmas will be as happy
as my fond wishes would make it
had they the power. Yours truly, Michael Davitt.

Inghinidhe na hÉireann

Portrait of Maud Gonne by Sarah Purser, 1898

She sketched you in pastels, over coffee
while you were staying in Mespil House.
You had fractured an arm and tiresome Yeats
was to visit. The sling is nowhere to be seen

and all personal adornment is gone.
Instead, the skin tone of this half-profile
is all about height. You were over six-foot tall,
but here, stature's in the eyes, independence

of the mouth, lethal backbone in the gaze.
No matter that your hair is a dark flame
or the headpiece threatens full flight.
You have given birth twice and carry a pair

of baby booties hidden at the waistline –
and into that campaign for the rest of your life.

Two Portraits, Michael Davitt

Every inch the Russian Count,
in fur hat, sable-lined coat, and boots,

he posed for the camera at Kishinev,
intense gaze investigating the riven world

before him. Less than a year on, books
and paper brighten the desk next to quill and ink

where a hand waits at ease.
Brow deeply furrowed, eyes in a trance,

hair thinned at the crown, bow-tie askew,
weather-beaten aging face glowered:

Take my advice, don't take any side,
just live, and try to understand

the beauties of this world …
He was hardly to know that death

would spirit him away within weeks.
The noble statesman captured here

ruminates, listens, rests on no laurel,
considers the stony road: vision, effort, failure.

Legacies of Empire

i.m Michael Davitt

1.

'Can you create a sketch within the space
outlined in red pencil of Ireland with
"landlordism" become a kind of blight?
On second thoughts, a winged vulture,
that throws a shadow across the land.
The sketch be made in India ink,
to print well in photographic presses.'

2.

It was said by old people, who mind
the year he was born, that the starving
were found on the sides of roads,
in the fields, once or twice on the street.
Mothers with infants in their arms,
children, hand-in-hand with father,
sometimes a toy, a puppy in their grip,
all their belongings heaped on carts,
walked mile after mile barefoot
against the clock of an empty gut.

Brigantium

> *'My heart aches, and a drowsy numbness pains*
> *My sense, as though of hemlock I had drunk …'* — Keats

It held me in its grip. Alone in the park
in the last hour before sunset.
As if it were a magnet. That delicate scent.
Ivory blooms hung like upside-down lilies.

Miniature flamenco dresses with
cream flounces. Trumpets drop,
one by one across the grass.
Where in the world does it come from?

Not here above the harbour, with lit sails
on the water in the last brightness
where once a Roman fleet cast anchor,
discovered an earth greener

and maybe brought seeds?
How complicated things can get
when you look in the gathering dusk
and the sky all by itself makes a show

of saying goodbye to the day.
With one eye on the ancient city walls,
a tree stores a season's heat in its limbs,
without a word, trusts itself to the world.

21, rue Bonaparte

Hair in a chignon, she turned her back
on barred gates, a genteel upbringing,
walked away from frigid drawing room
and hunt balls, *a suitable man.*

A stone's throw from the Seine, fell in love
with steam and balm, the sun burning her gut:
l'ouevre belle est plus vrai que l'artiste.
She kept a life-long salon, conceived
rugs, chairs; a cliff-house at Roquebrune.

Maiden Voyage

As if she were
gliding aboard a liner

she came to blossom that year,
so elegant and assured,

a hat grandmother made
boxed for the wedding

when ice gashed
below sea-level
and a torrent burst in.

One mother locked below deck
settled her children in bed
with a story.

A brave illusion of safety
while the Atlantic churned the ship,
split the hull,

and she was plunged
into the black swell,
choking and swallowing

the throng that yawled
inside her head,
when an outstretched hand

strong and warm,
hauled her onto boards
stricken and too numb to scream.

Wounds

Fingers reach into peat
in the half light and draw
a tuft of sphagnum.
Green cushions
lift from roots –
a fibrous tangle
veined like linen strands,
combed of twigs,
leaves, bits of grit –

drop into jute sacks.
Knee deep, at the bog's edge,
women, old men, young scouts,
miles from home
gather until sleep,
to send to the depot.
Rinsed, dried, pressed flat,
moss reached the Front
behind lines of fire

at the casualty clearing station,
became a cure in the hands of Nurse
who cleaned wounds of mud,
shrapnel, pus;
pillowed the injured
head of someone's *dearest*,
stretchered from the blast,
absorbed the flow of blood.

Surgeons & Insurgents

Large as life she stands tall again in
green citizen army uniform,
once worn by comrade Michael Mallin,

a pistol trailing from her right hand,
close to the centre of the great hall
where a floor-full of men slept soundly

on polished boards, and snores drove women,
too excited to sleep, downstairs
searching for peace, dressed for action.

Painter's Model

i.m. Wally Neuzil

When she heard, the first time they met
at the café, that he'd pay her to sit –
unheard-of small-town girl, seventeen,
half-dressed before him, she felt her
whole body grow numb in the chair
from that still, brave posture. The first months

of wild-fire paint, skin white-hot under
lace collar and black dress, she lied
to her friends. He taught her the tango,
they moved out of town, to find space
together in the world. She became
the woman with red lips, tawny hair,

raised knees, black stockings, electric
sea-green eyes, head turned to one side,
magnetised by his hands, moving fast,
her heart galloping. She kept house,
framed prints, saw clients, sold new work,
paid the rent, slept alone,

young models by the door at all hours,
strange habits. When she heard that he was
not going to marry her, and met
someone else, she cried hard. He thought how
she would get over it, be mistress,
mesmerised by her hands packing up.

He did not know then that he would not
see her face again, except that
he painted them – *death and the maiden.*

Guinea Fowl

after Guinea, Umayyad, Sicily, 9–11th century

Cast in bronze, a stocky bird,
the fretted design, tiny holes for dots,

becomes the entire flock let loose from the barn.
Polka-dot grey feathers, an exotic chiffon print,

red wattles and white heads chase grain
scattered by the slender wrist

of a newly-wed. She stands in the orchard
between crab apple and pear,

homesick for Skule Hill,
flowery bib over her dress,

cradling the empty meal bucket,
coaxing African birds, 'chook', 'chook'.

Sharp, vigilant eyes and raspy squawks
protect chickens from the fox

where they perch, on a garden wall
pock-marked by the Black-and-Tans.

Digital Archive

Like the *Pied Piper of Hamelin*,
Madam wheels her bicycle followed by
a tenement street of children;

with Dell Larkin at the soup kitchen
she stirs the pot, during the Lockout;
by her cell window in Kilmainham

she prays for the young life taken
by gunshot; on Holloway Prison paper
practises her new signature.

Binn Éadair, En Plein Air

after Sarah Purser's, 'The Little Regatta, Howth, 1923'

That cairn she chose, catching her breath,
set an easel up, sun warming her back.
She paints the sky beyond her brush,
an oak tree's lone shadow,
that green hillside, opening out
and down into a summer's day.

She takes the view, or it takes her:
lighthouse and harbour –
a line of boats just putting out –
Ireland's Eye beyond the strait,
white sails mapping the Sound,
half-lost in mist and breaking light
towards Lambay. And rising from

southerly wind, a fragile peace,
our country free, this fond world
that no money can buy, not then or now,
and there again the warning bell,
her hours extend in pungent reek of oils,
and song of skylarks lifting from the heath.

Harry Clarke's *Gobnait*

> *'I do not feel the full soul of the artist is manifested*
> *until he can let light pour through his design.' – AE*

She stands, a legendary queen in profile,
long red hair, blanched face, a shimmering cloak,
patterned sapphire robes, lit by the afternoon sun.
Her right hand holds a silver staff,

her left, a honeycomb. She dreams of a sanctuary
modelled on a beehive to be built in the place
of nine white deer. Consider her now,
mute as she halts at the fire of a busy forge.

The music of metal hammering fills her ears,
and, close by the river, a wild snowy herd grazes
under oaks where she arrives after weeks

of weary searching in the cold, protected from thieves
by a swarm of bees. Hungry for a sign to set up home,
not believing her eyes, she begins to count, twice.

Magu and the Deer

In her left hand she took hold of one ear,
the horn, now warm and slippery to grasp,
and thong she'd strung round his wild neck
restraining him. She strolls back home
hauling the live protesting weight,
head high, breasts proud, back straight,
hair drawn tight from her noble brow,
through pines so tall she hears them creak.
Her skirt is of mail like any warrior,
she props two arrows on her shoulder,
the bow's a snake on her arm.
This path she reads with eyes closed.
Ears tuned to the night-forest, her lover's step,
in such shoes as these she'll walk on water.

Before the Solstice

Sometime after four
when the sun began to sink
low in the sky,
upstairs reading
she sensed night's touch,
his hold on her hips.

What happened next is
anyone's guess,
a trick of the light
inside her,
late afternoons
as darkness kneels

to the earth with
tender ceremony,
ear pressed to her lap,
claiming the fiery
colours of leaves
outside their window.

Adam

after Pierre de Montreuil vers 1260

His hair is curled and slightly red.
I had not thought of Adam as a Celt,
yet here he is, looking modestly down
from his pedestal, over arch of sternum,
right palm open, eternally receiving an apple.
The face is innocent as a girl's,
as if knowledge of intimacy
enlightens him. His eyes speak
no regret, though his earthly dream,
the one that
has taken him,
is nowhere to be seen
except in the soul's deep rapture,
gaze made flesh.

Eostre and Hare

The second she tilts her head
removes sunglasses,
I'm reminded

of how close I came
to a hare sitting tall
in the headland dawn

past Lissadell
motionless in long grass,

eyes of yellow amber
exposed on the uphill
of an oval, profile,

the span of a field in its gaze,
sight, sound, speed – entire being
tuned for escape.

Fledglings

Down the South Bull Wall, black guillemots
sat in a line on flat granite flags,
seven or eight– what a sight– the way
they flipped, one after the other, into air
as if a thread were pulled when the dog
fifty yards away, stopped and stared.
First, three in the water, then all
took flight over the side into the brine.
Around the lighthouse, a crescent
of fishermen, Polish, Chinese, Brazilian,
cast off the bulwark for mackerel.
On the way back, by the Half Moon,
flocks of dunlin stood on low rocks.
Buff-feathered parents nudged them off,
white-barred wings spreading.
They landed at the shore, then flew
into the air as if one body, gliding along
a breaker, changing formation.
Now on the estuary, in the flow,
three black guillemots bobbed about,
and low, and behold, down the quay wall
leaning out of her crevice-nest,
the mother bird called to them
as they trailed the youngest
that playfully dipped its head,
dived into the deep and surfaced.
She, all the while attentive, called them
off the swift, outgoing current
that threatened to sweep them away,
urged them, and called them in, to safety.

Sea Swallows

dip low over the samphire-sea
as if, one body –
white rhythm, a cast arrow –
they glide above the drowsy tideline,
flight, a woven pattern.

Nesting in pairs, they lay eggs
in slatted grooves of the pontoon,
moored in the Liffey estuary,
brood and feed garrulous young,
dive and pick off sprats,
fatten for migration.

August evenings, take-offs,
landings, test-flights become
flung translucent veils
tuning efficiency.
Flocks mark daylight,
dark hearts primed for signals,

lift from this shore,
above the rainy earth
drawn by a force
into unknown winds,
currents that spiral
wings over ocean,

winnowed by storms,
by hunger and cold,
on the same wavelength
under the rising moon.

Prodigal

i.

As our family gathers at her deathbed
for a third night, mother's voice
comes back to me: *a watched kettle
never boils.*

ii.

Little did she know
that she who, above all, hated travel
would be cared for in her last days
by a young nurse from Kerala
who checked her pulse through the night,
counted beats over one minute,
placed a dark, plaited head close to her ear
to ask: *Water, my dear? You want water?*

iii.

In the hours before she took her last breath,
I sat in darkness, her hand in mine,
and wondered if she knew she was dying,
if she could sense that the one
who was holding her hand was me.

Coral

An Aran sweater in deep coral?
Wool was kitten-fur at my fingertips.
Alpaca, all the way from Trujillo.
Slides of the women you taught
to knit, diamond, blackberry and cable
stitch, sitting cross-legged outside
thatched huts, peopled
the flock wallpaper. Sweaters
hung on lines, strung across
the back of a truck en route to *Sears,*
past rows of sand-coloured barrios
in Lima, were luxuries sold
to American tourists. *There's nowhere
so poor in Ireland.* I looked in awe
at Aran in blood-orange pink,
normally heavy and rough to my skin,
magically tamed, raglan-sleeved,
rib-necked, fine, turned cuffs.
My mother praised the hand
of *a beautiful even knitter with just
the right tension.* I hugged it
to my chest, vowed one day I'd visit
Cusco, Machu Picchu, hot springs
of the Inca, take the long journey
west, a stowaway, the single-file,
airless passage through Panama.

Women Only

At the Ladies Pond at Hampstead they sprawl
on the grass, women in bathing suits

and sunglasses, groups and pairs, lovers,
friends, one or two heads shaved, a few

dressed in black vests or twin-sets and pearls.
Late afternoon in May, the sun slants hot;

nobody wants to leave yet, summer ahead.
Gnats multiply in the shade under trees.

Sunday papers unread, women dive and swim
the full length of the pond,

gather around lifebelts anchored in the stream,
voices light with sensation. Eyes closed,

I see hawthorn, though this is London,
wild parsley around the fence; what I hear

above the din as someone surfaces from
cold brackish water is *Oh man!*

Nightingale's Song

Mother kept house like Nelly Dean
lit open fires, prepared warm meals,
proffered tea, tip-toed from the table
stacked with books for the week,
unable to speak the language I read,
wore sacrifice on her sleeve,
Don't let me disturb you,
respect tinged with ambiguity,
I never got the chance,
and anyway, life was already full
of drama and mystery,
thanks ever so much.

Yet, it was that curiosity she nursed
in me, not knowing where it would lead,
eager to bestow the universe denied her
at thirteen, not expecting –
the nightingale's song in Keats –
how the ethereal fastness
of some word-hoard became
a starlit firmament inside me.
Now I bustle about, bring fresh coffee
while my daughter studies,
and, when she is altered by chemistry
beyond me, she becomes herself – and free.

Riverrun

Standing on stage, mouth
a fluent river of sound,

your face, lifted to the light,
brow and cheekbones
pronounce a litany, *Calling all
downs. Calling all downs to dayne.
Array! Surrection!* The words,

a magnetic lair, shelter a girl
left to her own devices,
blinds drawn on her parent's room.
The frame of the bed is a tight-rope,
and she has launched herself out
in a bathing suit, arms
see-sawing wide, gaze fixed,

sole sliding forward
in ballet slippers on tautness
of wire, posed mid-flight
across the deep, dark drop,
breath held as she shifts weight
to pivot and balance the other foot
before all eyes in the circus tent
smelling of sawdust and sweat.

Tosca

Sweet words are titbits to the ginger hide.
Fed, she arches neck and spine
to his curved hand. Croons. Stippled
fur brushes his palm, her spine's
liquid to his touch. Tail in the air,
rising to dance, cat-paws knead cushions,
steep haunches flex. When he moves
away, she crouches low, meows him
to the door, sits tight, her eyes green
to slits. She's aware of each guest,
distances in the room between them,
shifts of tone, efforts at conversation.
Each filament of hair gauges
temperature. No one but she allows
who comes near. Woe betide one
who, unasked, draws close to where
she curls. She'll hiss and spit,
sink claws in the wrist, draw livid blood.

Traders

'Ar scáth a chéile a mhairimíd.' – proverb*

The card arrived in Chivers jelly,
one of forty-eight – *Wild Wisdom in Africa.*
Details on the back read: species, habitat, prey.
'Endangered' was not in the vocabulary.
The Great Rift Valley, Lake Tanganyika,
Victoria Falls, the Serengeti were
Safari parks, no longer colonies.
The deck was brought to school to trade.
'Monkey', 'zebra', 'ostrich', maybe all three,
annoyingly paid for a 'croc' or 'lion.'
It must have been where 'vulture' first
peered innocuously from a tree,
grey feathers camouflaged with leaves.

The Habit

We often met you on the passage –
our word for lane – on one of your strolls,
black, skirts billowing, the rosary
beads hanging from your waist
and the big crucifix hidden in deep
folds of worsted wool, over pale
plump ankles and laced leather
granny-heeled shoes. Reading lauds
or matins, you looked so alien
against the greenery of fields and hedge,
an immaculate wimple and veil,
your face framed by starched bands,
compared to us children in wellies and duds,
at home in the mucky paddock
fancying ourselves as Tommy Wade
on Dundrum at the Puissance event,
or Iris Kellet, in White City, in 1949.
Mostly you brought news first-hand,
from the local hospital where you nursed,
talked of a micro-climate, where plants
flourished of their own accord, fuchsia,
montbretia, calla lillies and hot pokers,
mapped for us Dingle, Mount Eagle,
Mizen and, *no frost ever in Schull.*

I Want to Hold Your Hand

Late Christmas Eve, out of the night
Uncle Eddie landed at our door

like Mercury come with lyre
from another world,

sack rustling across the threshold,
and handed to my mother

the ivory plastic guitar
for my unmusical brother.

Each Beatle face, and signature
was printed around the O of the resonator.

I swapped my "Penguin" racer,
fiddled with pegs and plucked

each string, learnt to play chords,
hum tunes, compare tones

on the fretboard to the busy strum
and cadences of plectrum.

John, Ringo, Paul and George smiled back,
from the poster on the bedroom wall.

The Hat

'Ceci n'est pas un chapeau' – René Magritte

Nary a glimpse of himself.
What she saw was the old felt hat
scored by the shape of his head
that kept the air cool about him –
drip seeds of hay and smelt
after a stinging day in the meadow –
bob up and down over the ditch,

appear to ramble by itself
between whitethorn hedgerows
thick with wild parsley, pollen, vetch.
In that season, skittish flocks
of small birds rose into branches
of a spreading ash, 'the first tree',
or twittered in the high green leaves

of a row of beech by the 'middle gap'.
The hat often wished it were a bird,
as did the woman, islanded by fields
with no one to talk to but herself.
Her steady eye followed the point
gliding to 'the turn' from the garden
where she lost sight of it entirely

and the hat went walkabout in the bog.
Inside the crown of his head was a map,
names that slid shyly off her tongue,
of fields that sprawled in darkness
around the dwelling at night: The Stand,
Loughlin's, Old Garden, The Pump,
Ring Fort, New Ranch, The Pound.

Like a Miniature Chillida

My grandfather's last lived
in the dark place under the stairs,
beside a jug of sour milk kept cool for baking,
the stink of boot polish, dusty cobwebs,
poison for rats. I knew what not to touch.
It was my job to reach the end of the shelf
to bring that heavy cast to the table
newly cleared and covered with newspaper.

He worked late, listening to the radio,
sewed tackle, mended shoes. Lifted tools
one by one from the box: knife, hammer,
awl, needle, tan soles already scored.
Unwinding the ball of hemp, he evened
out a length, licked ends together,
then with beeswax locked in his palm
like resin on a bow, drew threads taut.

Presence

Driving along the avenue one month after,
past Lombardy poplars – leafless –
new blonde fence posts
strung by his hands
with a double row of cable,
I glimpse his absence everywhere.
Though everything looks the same,
ions of the air have altered composition.

The tractor still stands in the yard
bucket aloft to the hay.
The herd cowers lonely against
the ditch in the black field.
Windswept swatches of pasture

glitter under sunshine.
This January morning
his wife combs icy leaves
from the gate into raw heaps
as his son at fifteen, slim gait
and lanky limbs, becomes
in the space of a month,
the young man, forking them

into the wheelbarrow.
His daughter shies away,
in some daydream
of him still here,
long black hair spun
brusquely from her face,
curled somewhere,
nowhere, in his old sweater.

Wave Riders

On wet sand a film of burnished
clouds, coral, ochre, blue,
mirrors a peaceful October sky
at the close of a stormy day
on the thundery coast
as surfers paddle out

in dripping shoals, entranced
to wait in lulls like seals,
where troughs begin.
Who am I? Why am I here?
One by one, they taste the fear,
forfeit time, then rise alone
to lips of towering waves,

take the drop clean along the face
and ride across the crested swell,
life-drawing on the Atlantic,
carve in the deep pocket
out of sight, as if lost
forever in the ocean
on whose silvery back they play,
oblivious of danger, sorrow,

everything but wonder,
as a body rides the green room –
fingers skimming brine –
is thrown under in a maelstrom
of saltwater swallowed in gulps,
the board tossed,
lungs screaming to burst.

Arrival

Is that the new baby?
Father enquired of Mother across the bonnet
getting out of the car,
discretion for once escaping him,

ears attuned, curious about life
over the wall. I stood listening.
A barely audible whinge broke the silence.
Somewhere an iron gate swung

open on its hinge. That was all,
though the penny dropped,
as Mother reached for the key
hidden high up in the stone slit by the porch.

That close thundery summer,
Sarah's round belly heaved
about her house, trailing a frank scent;
sweat, redcurrant leaves, humour.

She allowed me to touch through
her pink nylon apron, the baby's kicks
like wing-beats, under my palm
her curve, warm and firm as a drum.

The Chamber

One ear to chimney-breast, on bended knee, better to hear
trapped wing-beats, he prised ajar the black ornate
cast hood. Then slid his arm inside the flue
as though one gloved limb were deeply sunk

in hind-quarters of a cow, to guide the head *in utero*,
though here, no calf in hairy smear or bloody stink
was sensed. First, soot sprinkled rolled-up sleeve
of shirt; his thumb and fingers gripped wiry claws

and held. Down, gently, drew his haul into the room.
Dishevelled. Stained. Feathery mass weighed his hands.
He cupped the ample beating heart and walked.
The bird was fond of warmth, or slightly stunned.

For seconds brooded. Then, lifted wings and hopped
onto the window ledge. And flew. A freed white dove.

Notes

p. 32 Based on a letter from Michael Davitt to Sarah Purser, 19 December 1888. Manuscript Room, National Library of Ireland (NLI), Dublin.

p. 34 Photograph, Kishinev, February 1906, Michael Davitt Archive, Trinity College Dublin. William Orpen's Portrait of Michael Davitt, 1906, Dublin City Gallery The Hugh Lane, Dublin.

p. 35 Quotation from letter from Michael Davitt to Sarah Purser, 16 September 1890. Manuscript Room, National Library of Ireland (NLI), Dublin.

p. 36 Brigantium: Roman name for Betanzos in Galicia, Spain.

p. 37 Eileen Gray lived at 21, Rue Bonaparte, V1 Arr. Paris from 1907 until her death in 1976. "L'oeuvre belle est plus vrai que l'artiste" is quoted in *Eileen Gray: Her Life and Work,* Peter Adam, Schirmer/Mosel, Verlag, GmbH, 2009.

p. 40. *Surgeons & Insurgents* was the title of an exhibition in April 1916 on the role of the Royal College of Surgeons (RCSI) in the 1916 Rising.

p. 41. Walburga 'Wally' Neuzil was the muse of Austrian painter Egon Schiele.

p. 44 *Binn Éadair,* trans. hill of the oaks.

p. 45 St. Gobnait: one of the saints profiled in a Harry Clarke stained glass window in the Honan Chapel, Cork in 1916.

p. 46. Magu: a Chinese Taoist goddess with supernatural powers; a protector of women.

p. 49 Bede refers to an Anglo-Saxon goddess, Eostre of the spring, and April as 'Eostremonath'.

p. 56 "Calling all downs. Calling all downs to dayne. Array! Surrection!" James Joyce, *Finnegans Wake,* p. 593 , Faber & Faber Ltd, London, 1939.

p. 58 *Ar scáth a chéile a mhairimíd'* – proverb; 'Under the one shadow we live'.

ACKNOWLEDGEMENTS

Acknowledgements are due to the editors of the following anthologies and books where some of these poems, or versions of them, previously appeared:

'The Habit'/'L'habit' (and other poems), *Jeune Poésie d'Irlande: Poètes du Munster 1960–2015*, translated and selected by Clíona Ní Ríordaín et Paul Bensimon (Editions Illador, Versailles, 2015); 'O Halloran's Fort' in *Migrant Shores: Moroccan, Irish and Galician Poetry*, ed. by Manuela Palacios (Salmon Poetry, 2017); 'Coral' and 'The Habit' and in *Ex-sistere, Women's Mobility in Contemporary Irish, Welsh and Galician Literatures*, ed. María Jesús Lorenzo-Modia (Cambridge Studies, 2016); 'Orfeo', and 'Nocturne' (from 'Land League Cottage'), *fermata, An Anthology of Poetry & Music*, Ed. by poet, Eva Bourke, and writer/broadcaster, Vincent Woods (Artisan House, 2016); 'The Habit', and 'The Hat' in *Dream of a City, An Anthology of Contemporary Poetry from Limerick City of Culture 2014*, ed. Kevin Honan (Astrolabe Press, Dublin, 2014); 'A Marketable Craft', *Even the Daybreak, 35 Years of Salmon Poetry*, ed. Jessie Lendennie (Salmon Poetry, 2016); 'Harry Clarke's Gobnait' and 'The Habit' in *On De Banks, Cork City in Poems & Song*, ed. Alannah Hopkin (Collins Press, 2016); *If Ever You Go, A Map of Dublin in Poetry & Song*, eds. Pat Boran and Gerard Smyth (Dedalus Press, Dublin, 2014); *Femmes d'Irlande en poésie 1973–2013*, eds. Clíona Ní Ríordáin et Paul Bensimon (Éditions Caracterès 7, 2013); *Windharp, Poems of Ireland since 1916*, ed. Niall MacMonagle, (Penguin Books Ltd., 2016).

Thanks too to the editors of the following journals, newspapers and radio programmes:

'The Chamber' (Jan. 24th, 2015) and 'O'Halloran's Fort' (March 4th, 2017), *The Irish Times,* poetry ed. Gerard Smyth;

'Legacies of Empire', *Poetry Ireland Review* 123, 2017, ed., Eavan Boland; 'S-I-N-G-E-R', Eithne Hand producer and Evelyn Grant presenter of *Lyric FM Poetry File,* RTÉ Lyric FM 2018; 'Lá Fhéile Pádraig', 'Île de la Cité', and 'Wounds', *Sunday Miscellany*, Ed. Sarah Binchy, RTÉ Radio 1, 2014,16,17; 'Magu and the Deer', 'Adam', 'Sea Swallows', 'Before the Solstice', 'Wild Atlantic Way', 'Now I See Them Everywhere', are published in *Lute & Drum* (online) Issue 12, A Quarterly of the Arts, Ed. Ken Taylor, Durham, North Carolina 2018; 'S-I-N-G-E-R', *The Ogham Stone*, University of Limerick, 2017; 'Coral', *The Stony Thursday Book*, No. 12, A Collection of Contemporary Poetry ed. Paddy Bushe, 2013; 'Expectant', No. 14, ed. Mary O Donnell, 2015; 'Letter to Sarah Purser: 19.12.1888', No. 15, ed. John Davies, 2016; *The Herald*, Scotland, Poem of the Day, ed. Lesley Duncan, 2017 & 2018; *Cork Literary Review*, ed. Kathy D'Arcy, 2016; *Cuadernos del Matemático,* No. 49, traduccion de Luz Pichel, con la colaboración de Manuela Palacios, Les Cressons Bleus, Madrid, 2014; *Saint Paul Almanac*, eds. Fletcher and Kirkpatrick, Arcata Press, St Paul, Minnesota, 2014; *Metamorphic: 21st Century Poets Respond to Ovid*, eds. Nessa O'Mahony and Paul Munden, Recent Work Press, U. of Canberra, Australia, 2017.

My thanks to *Centre Culturel Irlandais*, and Sheila Pratschke then Director, for a residency in February and March of 2013. The opportunity to live in Paris was a source of inspiration in the writing of several poems in this collection. My thanks to Culture Ireland for funding my travel to America, and support for readings, in 2012, and to Cyprus in 2015.

Thanks too to *The Arts Council, An Comhairle Ealaíon* for a Bursary in Literature received in 2013.

In April, 2014, I was honoured to receive The Lawrence O'Shaughnessy Award for Irish Poetry from the University of

St Thomas, St. Paul, Minnesota. I am grateful to the patron for the trust, and to Thomas Dillon-Redshaw and James S. Rogers for their continued encouragement.

My thanks to the organisers of Ideogramma, Lily Michaelides and Nora Hadjisotiriou of the International Literary Festival 2015, in Nicosia, for the opportunity to participate.

Thanks to *Poetry International* (online), and the *Munster Literature Centre* for including a selection of my poems and a profile on the website; and to Christine Murray, editor of *POETHEAD*, who published my poems in *Contemporary Irish Women Poets, & An Index of Irish Women Poets* (online).

Sincere thanks to colleagues and writer friends, Renate Ahrens, Julie Parsons, Sheila Barrett and Cecilia McGovern for readings and encouragement over the years; to poets Jane Clarke, Jessica Traynor, Rosamund Taylor and Eithne Hand for their insight and encouragement; to Jonathan Williams for his generous copyediting. I appreciate very much the opportunity to attend *The Irish Seminar* lectures on the literature and history of Modernism, at O'Connell House in 2011, with thanks to Declan Kiberd.

I am grateful to Vivienne Roche for her *Climate Bell 3* sculpture image, and to Pat Boran of Dedalus Press for publishing *Daughters of the House* and for his attention to the poems.

Finally, my gratitude to Justin MacCarthy who has been a constant companion through my writing life.

www.ingramcontent.com/pod-product-compliance
Lightning Source LLC
LaVergne TN
LVHW041345080426
835512LV00006B/619